ISBN 978-1-397-36170-7
PIBN 10121683

Forgotten Books is a registered trademark of FB &c Ltd.
Copyright © 2018 FB &c Ltd.
FB &c Ltd, Dalton House, 60 Windsor Avenue, London, SW19 2RR.
Company number 08720141. Registered in England and Wales.

For support please visit www.forgottenbooks.com

Slavery and the Slave-Trade in the District of Columbia.

SPEECH OF HORACE MANN,

OF MASSACHUSETTS,

In the House of Representatives, February 23, 1849.

SLAVE-TRADE IN THE DISTRICT ILLEGAL.

Mr. Chairman:—There is a bill upon the Speaker's table which provides for abolishing the slave-trade in the District of Columbia. For three successive days we have tried in vain to reach it, in the order of business. Its opponents have baffled our efforts. Our difficulty is not in carrying the bill, but in reaching it. I am not without apprehension that the last sands of this Congress will run out, without any action upon the subject. Even should the bill be taken up, it is probable that all debate upon it will be suppressed by that sovereign silencer,—the previous question. Hence I avail myself of the present opportunity, as it is probably the only one I shall have, during the present session, to submit my views upon it.

I frankly avow, in the outset, that the bill provides for one part only of an evil, whose remedy, as it seems to me, is not only the object of a reasonable desire, but of a rightful and legal demand. The bill proposes the abolition, not of slavery, but only of the slave trade in the District of Columbia. My argument will go to show that within the limits of this District, slavery ought not to exist in fact, and does not exist in law.

STATE OF THINGS IN THE DISTRICT.

Sir, in the first plac·, let us inquire what is the state of things in this District on this subject. The gentleman from

Indiana, [Mr. R. W. Thompson,] who addressed us a few days since, used the following language :

"What is the slave trade in the District of Columbia? I have heard a great deal said about 'slave pens,'—about slaves sold at auction,—and about stripping the mother from the child, and the husband from the wife. These things may exist here, but I do not know of them. Since I have been in the habit of visiting the District,—which is from my boyhood, —I have never seen a negro sold here,—I have never seen a band of negroes taken off by the slave trader. I do not remember that I have ever seen the slave trader himself. I know nothing of the 'slave pen' that is so much talked about. It may be here, however, and these things may happen every day before the eyes of gentlemen who choose to hunt them up, but for myself, I have no taste for such things."

Now, sir, if the gentleman means to say that he has no personal knowledge of "slave pens" and of the slave traffic in that District, this is one thing ; but if he means to deny or call in question the existence of the traffic itself, or of the dens where its concentrated iniquities make up the daily employment of men, that is quite another thing. Sir, from the western front of this Capitol, from the piazza that opens out from your Congressional Library, as you cast your eye along the horizon and over the conspicuous objects of the landscape,—the President's Mansion, the Smithsonian Institution, and the site of the Washington Monument, you cannot fail to see the horrid and black receptacles where human beings are penned like cattle, and kept like cattle, that they may be sold like cattle—as strictly and literally so as oxen and swine are kept and sold at the Smithfield shambles in London, or at the cattle fair in Brighton. In a communication made during the last session, by the Mayor of this city, to an honorable member of this House, he acknowledges the existence of slave pens here. Up and down the beautiful river that sweeps along the western margin of the District, slavers come and go, bearing their freight of human souls to be vended in this market-place; and after they have changed hands, according to the forms of commerce, they are re-transported—the father of a family to go, perhaps, to the rice fields of South Carolina, the mother to the cotton fields of Alabama, and the children to be scattered over the sugar plantations of Louisiana or Texas.

NOTORIOUS FACTS.

Sir, it is notorious that the slave traders of this District advertise for slaves in the newspapers of the neighboring counties of Maryland, to be delivered in any numbers at their slave pens in this city; and that they have agents, in the city and out of it, who are engaged in supplying victims for their shambles. Since the gentleman from Indiana was elected to this Congress, and, I believe, since he took his seat in this Congress, one coffle of about sixty slaves came, chained and driven into this city; and at about the same time another coffle of a hundred. Here they were lodged for a short period, were then sold, and went on their returnless way to the engulphing South.

Sir, all this is done here under our own eyes, and within hearing of our own ears. All this is done now, and it has been done for fifty years,—ever since the seat of the National Government was established in this place, and ever since Congress, in accordance with the Constitution, has exercised "*exclusive* legislation" over it. But the gentleman from Indiana, though accustomed to visit this District from his boyhood, has "never seen a negro sold here;" he has "never seen a band of negroes taken off by the slave trader;" he "does not remember to have seen the slave trader himself;" he knows "nothing of the slave pen that is so much talked about." Sir, the eye sees, not less from the inner than from the outer light. The eye sees what the mind is disposed to recognize. The image upon the retina is nothing, if there be not an inward sense to discern it. The artist sees beauty; the philosopher sees relations of cause and effect; the benevolent man catches the slightest tone of sorrow; but the insensate heart can wade through tears and see no weeping, and can live amidst groans of anguish, and the air will be a nonconductor of the sound. I know a true anecdote of an American gentleman who walked through the streets of London with a British nobleman; and being beset at every step of the way by squalid mendicants, the American, at the end of the excursion, adverted to their having run a gauntlet between beggars. "What beggars?" said his lordship, "*I have seen none.*"

"NO TASTE FOR SUCH THINGS."

But the gentleman from Indiana says, "but for myself, I have no taste for such things." His taste explains his vision.

Suppose Wilberforce and Clarkson had had no " taste " for quelling the horrors of the African slave trade. Suppose Howard and Mrs. Fry to have had no "taste" for laying open the abominations of the prison-house, and for giving relief to the prisoner. Suppose Miss Dix to have had no " taste" for carrying solace and comfort and restoration to the insane. Suppose the Abbe L'Eppe to have had no " taste " for teaching deaf mutes; or the Abbe Hauy for educating the blind ; or M. Seguin and others for training idiots; and for educing docility and decency and a love of order from those almost imperceptible germs of reason and sense, that barely distinguish them from the brutes! Suppose these things, and in what a different condition would the charities and the sufferings of the world have been! Herod had no " taste" for sparing the lives of the children of Bethlehem, and of all the coasts thereof; and doubtless he could have said, with entire truth, that he never heard the voice, in Rama, of lamentation and weeping and great mourning; nor saw, among all the mothers of Syria, any Rachel weeping for her children and refusing to be comforted, because they were not. But, sir, just in proportion as the light of civilization and Christianity dawns upon the world, will men be found who have a "taste" for succouring the afflicted and for righting the wronged. It was the clearest proof of the Great Teacher's mission, that he had " a taste" for going about, doing good.

EVEN UNCIVILIZED COUNTRIES IN ADVANCE OF US.

During the last fifty years, and especially during the last half of these fifty years, the world has made great advances in the principles of liberty. Human rights have been recognized, and their practical enjoyment, to some extent, secured. There is not a government in Europe, even the most iron and despotical of them all, that has not participated in the ameliorations which characterize the present age. A noble catalogue of rights has been wrested by the British Commons from the British nobility. France and Italy have been revolutionized. Even the Pope of Rome, whose power seemed as eternal as the hills on which he was seated, has sunk under the shock. Prussia, and all the Germanic Powers, with the exception of Austria, have been half revolutionized ; and even the icy despotisms of Austria and Russia are forced to relent under those central fires of liberty which burn forever in the human heart, as the central fires of the earth burn forever at its core. Great Britain has abolished African slavery throughout all her realms. France has declared that any one who shall voluntarily become the owner of a slave, or shall voluntarily continue to be the owner of a slave cast upon him by bequest or inheritance, shall cease to be a citizen of France. Denmark has abolished slavery wherever it existed in her possessions. The Bey of Tunis, acting under the light of the Mohammedan religion, has abolished it. The priests of Persia declare the sentiment to have come by tradition from Mohammed himself, "that the worst of men is the seller of men." Not only all civilized nations, but the half-civilized, the semi-barbarous, are acting under the guidance of the clearer light and the higher motives of our day. But there is one conspicuous exception ; there is one government which closes its eyes to this increasing light ; which resists the persuasion of these ennobling motives; which, on the grand subject of human liberty and human rights, is stationary and even retrogades, while the whole world around is advancing; sleeps while others are awaking; loves its darkness while all others are aspiring and ascending to a purer air and a brighter sky. This government, too, is the one which is the most boastful and vainglorious of its freedom; and if the humiliating truth must be spoken, this government is our own. In regard to slavery and the slave trade, in this District, where we possess the power of exclusive legislation, we stand where we stood fifty years ago. Not a single ameliorating law has been passed. In practice, we are where we were then; in spirit, there are proofs that we have gone backwards.

There are now on the surface of the globe two conspicuous places,—places which are attracting the gaze of the whole civilized world,—whither men and women are brought from great distances to be sold, and whence they are carried to great distances to suffer the heaviest wrongs that human nature can bear. One of these places is the coast of Africa, which is among the most pagan and benighted regions of the earth ; the other is the District of Columbia, the capital and seat of Government of the United States.

As far back as 1808 Congress did what it could to abolish the slave trade on the coast of Africa. In 1820 it declared the foreign slave trade to be piracy ; but on the 31st of January, 1849, a bill was introduced into this House to abolish the domestic slave trade in this District,—here, in the centre and heart of the nation,—and seventy-two Representatives voted against it,—voted to lay it on the table, where, as we all know, it would sleep a dreamless sleep. This was in the House of Representatives. It is well known that the Senate is still more resistant of progress than the House; and it is the opinion of many that even if a bill should pass both House and Senate, it would receive the Executive veto. By authority of Congress, the city of Washington is the Congo of America.

STILL MORE DEGRADING CONTRAST.

But, still more degrading than this, there is another contrast which we present to the whole civilized world. The very slaves upon whom we have trodden have risen above us, and their moral superiority makes our conduct ignominious. Not Europeans only, not only Arabians and Turks, are emerging from the inhumanity and the enormities of the slave traffic; but even our own slaves, transplanted to the land of their fathers, are raising barriers against the spread of this execra· ble commerce. On the shores of Africa, a republic is springing up, whose inhabitants were transplanted from this Egypt of bondage. And now look at that government which these slaves and descendants of slaves have established, and contrast it with our own. They discard the institution of Slavery, while we cherish it. A far greater proportion of their children than of the white children of the slave States of this Union, are at school. In the metropolis of their nation, their flag does not protect the slave traffic, nor wave over the slave mart. Would to God that the very opposite of this were not true of our own. Their laws punish the merchandise of human beings; our laws sanction and encourage it. They have erected, and are erecting, fortifications and military posts along the shores of the Atlantic, for seven hundred miles, to prevent pirates from invading the domain of their neighbors, and kidnapping people who, to them, are foreign nations. We open market-places here, at the centre of the nation, where; from seven hundred miles of coast, the sellers may come to sell, and where the buyers may come to buy, and whence slaves are carried almost as far from their birth-place as Africa is from America. The Governor of Liberia has lately made a voyage to England and France, and entered into treaties of amity and commerce with them; and he has obtained naval

the same time we are affording guaranties to the same traffic.
Virginia and Maryland are to the Slave Trade what the inte-
rior of Africa once was. The Potomac and the Chesapeake
are the American Niger and Bight of Benin; while this District is the great Government barracoon, whence coffles are
driven across the country to Alabama or Texas, as slave ships
once bore their dreadful cargoes of agony and wo across the
Atlantic. The very race, then, which were first stolen,
brought to this country, despoiled of all the rights which God
had given them, kept in bondage for generations, at last, after
redeeming themselves, or being restored to their natural
liberty in some other way, have crossed the ocean, established
a government for themselves, and are now setting us an example which should cause our cheeks to blister with shame.

CHARLES BROWN'S APOLOGY—"SLAVES BETTER OFF."

Sir, there is an idea often introduced here and elsewhere,
and made to bear against any restriction of Slavery, or any
amelioration of the condition of the slave, which I wish to
consider. It was brought odiously and prominently forward
the other day, by the gentleman from Pennsylvania, (Mr.
CHARLES BROWN.) The idea is, that the slaves are in a better
condition in this country than they would have been at home.
It is affirmed that they are brought under some degree of civil-
izing and humanizing influences amongst us, which they
would not have felt in the land of their fathers.

Let us look, first, at the philosophy of this notion, and then
at its morality. All those who use this argument as a defence
or a mitigation of the evils of Slavery, or as a *final cause* for
its existence, *assume* that if the present three million slaves
who now darken our southern horizon, and fill the air with
their groans, had not been here in their present state of
bondage, they would have been in Africa, in a state of paganism. Now, the slightest reflection shows that this as-
sumption has no basis of truth. Not one of them all would
now have been in existence, if their ancestors had not been
brought to this country. And, according to the laws of population operative among barbarous nations, there are now
just as many inhabitants,—pagans, cannibals, or what you

n Africa, as there would have been if the spoiler

into bondage. Among savage nations, or nomadic tribes, the population equals the means of subsistence. Take away two,

immediately supplied. The population keeps up to the level of the production. Among such people, there is always a tendency to increase faster than the means of living increase. Take away a part of them, and this tendency to increase takes effect by its own vigor, it executes itself. It is like a bow that unbends, or a spring that uncoils, as soon as an external pressure is removed. Dam up a fountain, and the weight of the accumulating strata will eventually check the outflow from the spring. So it is of a savage population. Of them the Malthusian theory is true.

ABSURDITY OF THE PLEA.

And how infinitely absurd and ridiculous is the plea that the slaves are better off here *than* THEY *would have been in Africa!* Go out into the streets of this city, and take the first one you meet,—perhaps he is a mulatto. But for being here, he would have been a mulatto in the middle of Africa, would he? Take them all,—mulatto, mestizo, zambo, and all " the vast variety of man," so far as color is concerned,—and if they had not their existence here, they would have had it in Africa! This is the doctrine. Would they have had the same American names also? Would they have spoken the same language, and worn cotton grown on the same fields? The last is just as certain as the first. It is all more silly than the repinings of the silly girls who grieved because their mother had not married a certain rich suitor, whose addresses in early life she had rejected; for then, said they, how rich *we* should have been! No, not one of these three millions of men, women and children, would have been in existence in Africa. All the crime of their kidnapping; all the horrors of the middle passage; all their sufferings for two centuries, or six generations; and all the calamities that are yet to grow out of their condition,—all these crimes and agonies are gratuitous crimes and agonies. There is no recompense or palliation for them. They have been added unnecessarily and remorselessly to the amount of human guilt and suffering for which the white race must answer in the day of account.

nding the

an egregious fallacy. If they were to be sent *back* whence they came, it would not be to Africa, but to nonentity.

If the ancestors of the present three millions of slaves had
had never been
services, their
white laborers, by men
of the Caucasian race,—by freemen. Instead of the three million slaves, of all colors, we should doubtless now have at least three million white, free-born citizens, adding to the real prosperity of the country, and to the power of the Republic. If the South had not had slaves to do their work for them, they would have become ingenious and inventive like the North, and would have enlisted the vast forces of nature in their service,—wind and fire and water and steam and lightning, the mighty energies of gravitation and the subtle forces of chemistry. The country might not have had so gaudy and ostentatious a civilization as at present, but it would have had one infinitely more pure and sound.

INHUMANITY OF THE PLEA.

But admit the alleged statement, absurd and false as it is; admit that these three millions of slaves would have belonged to Africa if they had not belonged to America,—that they would have been born of the same fathers and mothers there as here, so that those of them who are American mulattoes would have been Ethiopian mulattoes; and admit, further, that their present condition is better than the alternative condition alleged,—and what then? Is your duty done? Is it enough if you have made the condition of a man or of a race a little better; or any better, if you have not made it as much better as you can? What standard of morals do gentlemen propose to themselves? If a fellow-being is suffering under a hundred diseases, and we can relieve him from them all, what kind of benevolence is that which boasts of relieving him from one, and permits him to suffer under the other ninety-and-nine? By the law of nature and of God, the slave like every other man, is entitled to life, liberty, and the pursuit of happiness; he is entitled to his earnings,—to the enjoyment of his social affections,—to the development of his intellectual and moral faculties,—to that cultivation of his religious nature which shall fit him, not merely to feel, but reason of righteousness; temperance, and a judgment to come ; he is entitled to all these rights, of which he has been cruelly despoiled ; and when he catches some feeble glimmering of some of them, we withhold the rest, and defend ourselves and

in some other country, or in some other condition. Suppose the Samaritan had bound up a single wound, or relieved a single pang of the bleeding wayfarer who had fallen among thieves, and then had gone to the next inn and boasted of his benevolence. He would only have shown the difference between a "good Samaritan" and a "bigot Samaritan." The thieves themselves might have done as much.

But there is another inquiry which the champions of Slavery have got to answer before the world and before Heaven. If American slaves are better off than native Africans, who is to be thanked for it? Has their improved condition resulted from any purposed plan, any well-digested, systematized measure, carefully thought out, and reasoned out, and intended for their benefit? Not at all. In all the Southern statute books, and legislative records there is no trace of any such scheme. Laws, judicial decisions, the writings of political economists—all treat the slave as a thing to make money with. Agricultural societies give rewards for the best crops. Horse-jocky societies improve the fleetness of the breed for the sports of the turf. Even the dogs have professional trainers. But not one thing is done to bring out the qualities of manhood that lie buried in a slave. Look through the Southern statute books and see what Draconian penalties are inflicted for teaching a slave to read,—see how he is lashed for attending a meeting to hear the word of God. On every highroad patrols lie in wait to scourge him back, if he attempts to visit father, mother, wife, child, or friend, on a neighbouring plantation. By day and by night, at all times and everywhere, he is the victim of an energetic and comprehensive system of measures, which blot out his senses, paralyze his mind, degrade and brutify his nature, and suppress the instinctive workings of truth, generosity, and manhood in his breast. All the good that reaches him is in defiance of these privations and disabilities. If any light penetrates to his soul, it is because human art cannot weave a cloud dense and dark enough to be wholly impervious to it. There are some blessings which the goodness of God will bestow in spite of human efforts to intercept them. It is these only which reach the slave. And after having built up all barriers to forbid the access of improvement; after having sealed his senses by ignorance, and more than half obliterated his faculties by neglect and perversion, the oppressor turns round, and because there are some scanty, incidental benefits growing out of the very deplorableness of his condition, he justifies himself before the world and claims the approval of Heaven, because the slave is better off here than *he* would be in Africa. Sir, such an argument as this is would be an offence to Heaven. I consider it to be as much worse than Atheism as Christianity is better. And when such an argument comes from a gentleman belonging to a free state; when it comes from the gentleman from Pennsylvania, (Mr. Brown,) from a representative of the city of William Penn; when he, without motive, without inducement, offers such a gratuity to the devil, I can account for it only on the principle of the man who, having a keen relish for the flesh of swine, said he wished he were a Jew, that he might have the pleasure of eating pork and committing a sin at the same time.

REFINED ATROCITY OF THE SLAVE SYSTEM.

But the subject presents a still more painful aspect. How are slaves made better, and from what motives are they made better in this country? It is no secret that I am about to tell. There are certain virtues and sanctities which increase the pecuniary value of certain slaves; and there are certain vices and debasements which increase the market price of others. If a master wishes to repose personal confidence in his slave, he desires to have him honest and faithful to truth. But if he desires to make use of him to deceive and cajole and defraud, then he wishes to make him cunning and tricky and false. If the master trains the slave to take care of his own children, or of his favourite animals, then he wishes to have him kind; but if he trains him for a tasker or a field overseer, then he wishes to have him severe. Now, it is in this way that some of the Christian attributes of character, being directly convertible into money or money's worth, enhance the value of a slave. Hence, it is said in advertisements that a slave is pious, and, at the auction block, the hardened and heartless seller dwells upon the Christian graces and religious character of some slave, with the unction of an Apostle. The purchaser sympathizes, and only desires to know whether the article be a real or a sham Christian. If mere bones and muscles compacted into human shape be worth five hundred dollars, then, if the auctioneer can warrant the subject to have the meekness of Moses and the patience of Job, the same article may be worth seven hundred. If the slave will forgive injuries not merely seventy times seven, but injuries inflicted all his life long, then an additional hundred may be bid for him. If he possesses all the attributes of religion and piety, the endurance of a hero, the constancy of a saint, the firmness of a martyr, the trustingness of a disciple,—all except those which go to make him feel like a man,—then that which as mere bone and muscle was worth five hundred dollars, is now worth a thousand. Sir, is not this selling the Holy Spirit? Is not this making merchandise of the Saviour? Is not this the case of Judas selling his Master over again, with the important exception of the remorse that made the original culprit go and hang himself? But suppose the case to be that of a woman; suppose her ability to work and capacity for production to be worth five hundred dollars; suppose, in addition to this, she is young and sprightly and voluptuous; suppose the repeated infusion of Saxon blood has almost washed the darkness from her skin; and suppose she is not unwilling to submit herself to the libertine's embrace; then, too, that which before was worth but five hundred dollars, will now bring a thousand. And thus infernal as well as celestial qualities are coined into money, according to the demands of the market and the uses of the purchaser.

Now, it is only in some such incidental way, and with regard to some individuals, that it can be said, that their condition is better here than it would be in Africa. And this improvement, where it exists, is not the result of any system of measures designed for their benefit, but is the product of selfish motives, turning godliness into gain; and where more gain or more gratification can be obtained by the debasement, the irreligion, the pollution of the slave, there the instincts of chastity, the sancity of the marriage relation, the holiness of maternal love, are all profaned to give security and zest to the guilty pleasures of the sensualist and debauchee. There are individual exceptions to what I have said,—exceptions, which amid surrounding iniquity shine "like a jewel in an Ethiop's ear," but they are exceptions. Laws, institutions, and the prevailing public sentiment are as I have described.

Pennsylvania (Mr. Brown) not only as utterly unsound and
phemous in its conclusions.
Common blasphemy seldom reaches beyond exclamation. It
is some fiery outburst of impious passion, that flashes and ex-
pires. But the gentleman reasons it out coolly. His is argu-
mentative blasphemy, borrowing the forms of logic that it
may appear to have its force, and transferring it from the
passions to the intellect, to give it permanency.

DEFENCE OF MASSACHUSETTS.

· But the gentleman from Pennsylvania retorts upon Massachusetts, and refers to certain things in her history which
he regards as disreputable to her. In this, he has been fol-
lowed by the gentleman from Virginia, (Mr. Bedinger,) who
has poured out a torrent of abuse upon my native State, and
who has attempted to fortify his own intemperate accusations
from a Pro-Slavery pamphlet which has been profusely scattered about this house within a few days past, and which is
not merely full of falsehoods, but is composed of falsehoods;
so that if one were to take the false assertions and the false
arguments out of it, there would be nothing but the covers
left.* Sir, I am very far from arrogating for Massachusetts
all the merits and the virtues which she ought to possess. I
mourn over her errors, and would die to reform, rather than
spend one breath to defend them. The recital of her offences
can fall more sadly upon no ear than upon my own. But it
is as true of a State as of an individual, that repentance is the
first step towards reformation. Massachusetts has committed
errors; but when they were seen to be errors, she discarded
them. She once held slaves; but when she saw that Slavery
was contrary to the rights of man and to the law of God, she
emancipated them. She was the first government in the
world, ancient or modern,—to abolish slavery wherever she
had power to do so. This is an honor that no rival can ever
snatch from her brow. Once, I say it with humiliation,—she
was engaged in the Slave Trade. But all the gold that could
be earned by the accursed traffic, though spent in the splen-

_* Lecture on the North and South. Delivered in College Hall,
January 16, 1849, before the Young Mens' Mercantile Library
Association of Cincinnati. By Elwood Fisher._

dors of luxury and the seductions of hospitality, could not save the trader himself from infamy and scorn; and I am sure I am right in saying that the Slave Trade ceased to be conducted by Massachusetts merchants and to be carried on in Massachusetts ships, from Massachusetts ports, before it was abandoned by the merchants and discontinued in the ships and from the ports of any other commercial State or nation in the world. This, too, is an honor, which it will be hers, through all the immortality of the ages, alone to wear. But Massachusetts, it is still said, has her idolaters of Mammon in other forms. It is charged upon her that many of her children still wallow in the sty of intemperance; that her spiritualism runs wild in religious vagaries; and that something of the old leaven of persecution still clings to her heart. In vindicating what is right, I will not defend what is wrong. I cannot deny,—would to God that I could—that we still have vices and vicious men amongst us. There are those there, as elsewhere, who if they were to hear for the first time of the River of Life flowing fast by the throne of God, would instinctively ask, whether there were any millsites on it. There are those there, as elsewhere, whose highest aspirations for Heaven and for happiness, whether for this life or for another, are a distillery and a sugar-house, with steam machinery to mix the products. There, as elsewhere, are religionists who are quick to imitate the Saviour when he strikes, but despise his example when he heals.

But sir, let me say this for Massachusetts, that whatever sins she has committed in former times—whatever dissenters she may have persecuted, or witches she may have hanged, or Africans she may have stolen and sold, she has long since abandoned these offences, and is bringing forth fruits meet for repentance. And is a state to have no benefit from a statute of limitations? Is a crime committed by ancestors to be for ever imputed to their posterity? This is worse than non-forgiveness; it is making punishment hereditary. Sir, of these offences, Massachusetts has repented and reformed; and she is giving that noblest of atonements or expiations, which consists in repairing the wrongs that have been done; and where the victim of the wrong has himself passed away, and is beyond relief, then in paying, with large interest, the debt to humanity, which the special creditor is no longer present to receive, by seeking out the objects of want and suffering, wherever they may be found. Sir, our accusers unconsciously do us the highest honor, when, in their zeal to malign us, they seek for historical reproaches. If they could find present offences wherewith to upbraid us, they would not exhume the past. But they condemn themselves, for they show that even the resuscitation of the errors of the dead gives them more pleasure than a contemplation of the virtues of the living. One thing is certain, the moment the other states shall imitate our present example, they will cease to condemn us for past offences. The sympathy for a common desire for improvement will destroy the pleasure of crimination.

And where, I ask, on the surface of the earth, is there a population of only eight hundred thousand, who are striving so earnestly, and doing so much to advance the cause of humanity and civilization, as is doing by the people of Massachusetts? Where else where universal suffrage is allowed, is a million of dollars voted every year, by the very men who have to pay it, for the public, free education, of every child in the state? Where else, by such a limited population, is another million of dollars voted, and paid each year, for the salaries of clergymen alone? Where else, where the population is so small, and natural resources so few and scanty, is still another million of dollars annually given in charity?—the greater portion of which is sent beyond their own borders, flows into every State of the Union, and leaves not a nation on the globe, nor an island in the sea unwatered by its fertilizing streams. Look into the statute book of Massachusetts for the last twenty years, and you will see how the whole current of her legislation has set in the direction of human improvement—for succoring disease or restoration from it, for supplying the privations of nature, for reclaiming the vicious, for elevating all—a comprehensiveness of scope that takes in every human being, and an energy of action that follows every individual with a blessing to his home. When others will abandon their offences, then let the remembrance of them be blotted out.

But, sir, I think it proper to advert to the fact, that I have had other proofs, during the present session of Congress, of the same spirit of crimination and obloquy, which was so fully developed in the speeches of the gentleman from Pennsylvania (Mr. Brown) and the gentleman from Virginia (Mr. Bedinger.) Through the post-office of the House of Representatives, I have been in the regular receipt of anonymous letters, made up mainly of small slips cut from newspapers printed at the North, describing some case of murder, suicide, robbery or other offence. These have been arranged under the heads of different States—Ohio, Pennsylvania, New York, Connecticut, &c., and accompanied, in the margin, with rude drawings of a schoolbook or a schoolhouse, and all referred to common schools, as to their source. Two only, of the whole number thus collected, originated in Massachusetts, and one of these was a case of suicide, committed by a man who had become insane from the loss of his wife. Which of these events, in the opinion of my anonymous correspondent, constitutes the crime—whether the bereavement that caused the insanity, or the suicide committed in one of its paroxysms—I am unable to say. Now, what satisfaction a man could have in referring offences against law and morality to the institution of public schools, when he must have known that the very existence of the offences only proves that education has not yet done its perfect work, I cannot conceive. And what spite, either against an educational office which I once held, or against an institution which is worthy of all honor, could be so mean and paltry as to derive gratification from referring me to long lists of offences, only one of which was committed in my native State, I must leave for others to conjecture. Surely the author of these letters must have known little of common schools, and profited by them as little as he has known. Had he referred to any considerable number of crimes perpetrated in Massachusetts, I would take his letters home, and carry them into our public schools, and make them the text for a sermon, in which I would warn the children to beware of all crimes, and especially the meanness and wickedness which feels a complacency in the crimes of others, or can give a false paternity to them. And, sir, I should be sure of a response, for out of those schools there is going forth a nobler band of young men and women than ever before conveyed intelligence, virtue refinement, and renown, upon any people or community on the face of the globe.

ESPECIAL REASONS FOR ABOLITION IN THE DISTRICT.

But whatever may be said in mitigation or in condemnation of Slavery elsewhere, there are special reasons why it should be discontinued in this District. This District is the common property of the nation. Having power of exclusive legislation over it, we are all responsible for the institutions in it. While slaves exist in it, therefore, it can be charged upon the North that they uphold Slavery. This is unjust to us, because it places us before the world in the attitude of sustaining what we condemn. It wounds our moral and religious sensibilities, because we believe the institution to be cruel towards men, and sinful in the sight of Heaven; and yet we are made apparently to sanction it. It is like that species of injustice where a man is compelled by a tax to support a religion which he disbelieves, and to pay a hierarchy whom his conscience compels him to denounce. But the existence of Slavery here is not necessary to the faith or the practice of our Southern brethren. If they believe it to be a useful and justifiable institution, then they evince the sincerity of that belief by sustaining and perpetuating it at home. For this purpose, there is no necessity, of a crusade to propagate it, or sustain it elsewhere.

Look at the relation which we bear to it, in another respect. I have been taught from my earliest childhood that "all men are created equal." This has become in me not merely a conviction of the understanding, but a sentiment of the heart. This maxim is my principle of action, whenever I am called upon to act; and it rises spontaneously to my contemplations when I speculate upon human duty. It is the plainest corollary from the doctrine of the natural equality of man, that when I see a man, or a class of men, who are not equal to myself in opportunities, in gifts, in means of improvement, or in motives and incitements to an elevated character and exemplary life,—I say, it is the plainest corollary, that I should desire to elevate those men to an equality with myself. However far my own life may fall below the standard of Christianity and gentlemanliness, yet I hold it to be clear, that no man is a Christian or a gentleman, who does not carry about an habitual frame of mind which prompts him, as far as he has the means to do it, to instruct all the ignorance, to relieve all the privations, to minister to all the pains, and to supply all the deficiencies of those with whom he meets in the daily walks of life; and, so far as he is a man who wields influence, possesses authority, or exercises legislative power, he is bound to exert his gifts and his prerogatives for the amelioration and the improvement of his fellow-men. This is the lowest standard of duty that any one who aspires

2*

to be a Christian or a gentleman can set up for his guidance.
Now take the case of a man from the North, who has incorporated these views or any similitude of these views, into his
character, and who has occasion to visit this District. Suppose him to be elected and sent here as a member of Congress,
or to be appointed to a post in some of the departments, or to
visit this city on public business, or to come here from motives
of curiosity ; what is the sight which is inflicted upon him
when he first sets his foot within this common property of
the nation,—when he first enters this household, where the
head of the nation resides and directs? Sir, when he first
alights from the cars that bring him within your limits and
your jurisdiction, he beholds a degraded caste,—a race of
men whom God endowed with the faculties of intelligence,
but whom man has despoiled of the power of improving those
faculties, squalid in their garb, betraying ignorance in every
word they utter, uncultivated in their manners and their
tastes, fawning for favor, instead of standing erect like men
who are conscious of rights ; or, if they have outgrown servile
and sycophantic habits, then erring on the side of impudence
and insolence as much as they erred before on that of cring-
ing and servility. He repairs to his lodgings, and there, too,
all his moral sensibilities are shocked and outraged, by seeing
a class of men and women hopelessly degraded, cut off by
law and custom from all opportunity of emerging from their
debasement ; whom no talent, taste, or virtue can ever redeem
to the pleasures and the rights of social intercourse. He sees
men and women who are not degraded on account of the services they perform,—for " honor and shame from no condition rise,"—but degraded by the motive and spirit from which
the services are performed ; men and women who have no
inducements to industry and frugality, for their earnings will
all be seized by another ; who have no incentives to self-re-
spect, for they can never emerge from their mental condition ;
who are bereaved of all the wonders and glories of knowledge, lest under its expansions their natures should burst the
thraldom that enslaves them; and all whose manly qualities,
all whose higher faculties, therefore, are irredeemably and
hopelessly crushed, extinguished, obliterated, so that nothing
but the animal, which the master can use for his selfish purposes, remains.

" AMALGAMATION."

MR. BROADHEAD. Would you advance the slaves to an equal, social and political condition with the white race?

MR. MANN. I would give to every human being the best opportunity I could to develop and cultivate the faculties which God has bestowed upon him, and which, therefore, he holds under a divine charter. I would take from his neck the heel that has trodden him down; I would dispel from his mind the cloud that has shrouded him in moral night; I would remove the obstructions that have forbidden his soul to aspire ; and having done this, I would leave him, as I would leave every other man, to find his level,—to occupy the position to which he should be entitled by his intelligence and his virtues. I entertain no fears on the much dreaded subject of amalgamation. Legal amalgamation between the races will never take place, unless, in the changed condition of society, reasons shall exist to warrant and sanction it ; and in that case it will carry its own justification with it. But one thing I could never understand,—why those who are so horror-stricken at the idea of *theroretic* amalgamation, should exhibit to the world, in all their cities, on all their plantations, and in all their households, such numberless proofs of *practical* amalgamation. I never could see why those who arraign and condemn us at the North, so vehemently, because, as they say, we obtrude our prying eyes into what they call a " domestic " or " fireside " institution, should have no hesitation in exhibiting to the world, through all their borders, ten thousand and ten times ten thousand living witnesses that they make it a bedside institution. Multitudes of the slaves of the South bear about upon their persons a brand as indelible as that of Cain ; but the mark has been fastened upon them not for their own crimes but for their fathers'. In the complexion of the slave, we read the horrid history of the guilt of the enslavers. They demonstrate that the one race has been to the other, not the object of benevolence, but the victim of licentiousness.

SIGHTS IN WASHINGTON.

But to resume : When the visitor to this city from the North leaves his lodgings, and goes into the public streets, half the people whom he meets there are of the same degraded class. Their tattered dress and unseemly manners denote congenital debasement. Their language proclaims their ignorance. If you have occasion to send them on an errand, they cannot read the direction of a note, or a sign on a shop-board. Their ideas are limited within the narrowest range. They speak the natural language of servility, and they wear the livery of an inferior condition. The conviction of their deplorable state is perpetually forced upon the mind. You do not need their color to remind you of their degradation. Color, sir! They are oftentimes almost as white as ourselves. Sir, there is not a member of Congress who has not frequently seen some of his fellow members, in the spring of the year, with a jaundiced skin more sallow and more yellow than that of many a slave who is bought and sold and owned in this city. I have seen members of this House to whom I have been disposed to give a friendly caution to keep their " free papers " about their persons, lest suddenly, on the presumption from color, they should be seized and sold for runaway slaves. A yellow complexion here is so common a badge of slavery, that one whose skin is colored by disease is by no means out of danger. To enjoy security, a man must do more than take care of his life ; he must take care of his health. It is not enough to take heed to the meditations of his heart ; he must see also to the secretions of his liver.

But, sir, the stranger from the North visits the courts of justice in this city ; he goes into halls set apart and consecrated, even in the dark and half-heathenish periods of English history, to the investigation of truth and the administration of justice; but if he sees any specimens of the colored race there, he sees them only as menials. They cannot go there as witnesses. However atrocious the wrongs they may suffer in their own person and character, or in the person and character of wife or children, they cannot appeal to the courts to avenge or redress them. If introduced there at all, it is as a bale of goods introduced, or as an ox, or a horse is brought within their purlieus, for the purpose of trying some disputed question of identity or ownership. They go not as suitors, but as sacrifices. In the courts of law ; in the temples with which all our ideas of justice, of right between man and man, are associated ; where truth goes to be vindicated, where innocence flies to be avenged ;—in these courts, an entire portion of the human race are known, not as men, but as chattels, as cattle. Where, for them, is the Magna Charta, that the old barons wrested from King John? Is a whole race to be forever doomed to this outlawry? Are they forever to wear a "wolf's-head," which every white man may cut off when he pleases? Sir, it cannot be that this state of things will last forever? If all the rights of the black race are thus withheld from them, it is just as certain as the progress of time that they, too, will have their Runnymede, their Declaration of Independence, their Bunker Hill and their Yorktown.

Such, sir, are the sights that molest us when we come here from the North,—that molest us in the hotels, that molest us in the streets, that molest us in the courts, that molest us everywhere. But the week passes away, and the Sabbath comes,—the day of rest from worldly toils, the day set apart for social worship, when men come together, and by their mutual presence and assistance, lift up the hearts of each other in gratitude to God. But where now are the colored population, that seemed to be so numerous everywhere else? Have they no God?—Have they no interest in a Saviour's example and precepts? Have they no need of consolation, of faith in the Unseen, to help them bear up under the burdens and anxieties of life? Is their futurity so uncertain or so worthless that they need no guide to a better country, or that they can be turned off with a guide as ignorant and blind as themselves.

MORAL EVILS EVEN MORE ENORMOUS THAN THE PHYSICAL.

We go from the courts and the churches to the schools. But no child in whose skin there is a shadow of a shade of African complexion is to be found there. The channels are so cut that all the sacred and healing waters of knowledge flow, not to him, but by him. Sir, of all the remorseless and wanton cruelties ever committed in this world of wickedness and wo, I hold that to be the most remorseless and wanton which shuts out from all the means of instruction a being whom God has endued with the capacities of knowledge, and inspired with the divine desire *to know.* Strike blossom and beauty from the vernal seasons of the year, and leave it sombre and cheerless; annihilate the harmonies with which the birds of spring make vocal the field and the forest, and let exulting Nature become silent and desolate; dry up even those fountains of joy and gladsomeness that flow unbidden from the heart of childhood, and let the radiant countenance of youth become dull and stony like that of age ; do all this if you will, but withhold your profane hand from those creative sources of knowledge which shall give ever-renewing and ever-increasing delight through all the cycles of immortality, and which have the power to assimilate the finite creature more and more nearly to the infinite Creator. Sir, he who denies to children the acquisition of knowledge works devilish miracles. If a man destroys my power of hearing, it is precisely the same to me as though, leaving my faculty of hearing untouched, he had annihilated all the melodies and harmonies of the universe. If a man obliterates my power of vision, it is precisely the same to me as though he had blotted out the light of the sun, and flung a pall of darkness over all the beauties of the earth and the glories of the firmament. So, if a usurper of human rights takes away from a child the faculties of knowledge, or the means and opportunities to know, it is precisely the same to that child as though all the beauties and the wonders, all the magnificence and glory of the universe itself had been destroyed. To one who is permitted to know nothing of the charms and sublimities of science, all science is non-existent. To one who is permitted to know nothing of the historical past, all the past generations of men are a non-entity. To one whose mind is not made capacious of the future, and opened to receive it, all the great interests of futurity have less of reality than a dream. I say, therefore, in strict, literal, philosophical truth, that whoever denies knowledge to children, works devilish miracles. Just so far as he disables and incapacitates them from knowing, he annihilates the objects of knowledge ; he obliterates history ; he destroys the countless materials in the natural world that might, through the medium of the useful arts, be converted into human comforts and blessings ; he suspends the sublime order and progression of Nature, and blots out those wonderful relations of cause and effect that belong to her unchangeable laws. Nay, there is a sense in which such an impious destroyer of knowledge may be said to annihilate the Creator himself, for he does annihilate the capacity of forming an exception of that Creator, and thus prevents a soul that was created in the image of God from ever receiving the image it was created to reflect. Such a destroyer of knowledge dims the highest moral splendor of the universe. God is more to me than a grand and solitary Being, though refulgent with infinite perfections. Contemplated as enthroned in the midst of His works, His spiritual offspring in all the worlds he has formed become a multiplying glass, reflecting back the Original in all the profusion and countlessness of infinity. But when the wickedness of man cuts off entire generations and whole races from the capacity of reflecting back this radiant image of the Creator, then all that part of the universe where they dwell becomes black and revolting, and all that portion of the Mirror of Souls which was designed to reproduce and rekindle the glories of the Eternal, absorbs and quenches the rays which it should have caught and flamed with anew, and multiplied and returned. And still further, sir, I affirm, in words as true and literal as any that belong to geometry, that the man who withholds knowledge from a child not only works diabolical miracles for the destruction of good, but for the creation of evil also. He who shuts out truth, by the same act opens the door to all the error that supplies its place. Ignorance breeds monsters to fill up all the vacuities of the soul that are unoccupied by the verities of knowledge. He who dethrones the idea of Law, bids Chaos welcome in its stead. Superstition is the mathematical complement of religious truth ; and just so much less as the life of a human being is reclaimed to good just so much more is it delivered over to evil. The man or the institution, therefore, that withholds knowledge from a child, or from a race of children, exercises the awful power of changing the world in which they are to live, just as much as though he should annihilate all that is most lovely and grand in this planet of ours, or transport the victim of his cruelty to some dark and frigid zone of the universe, where the sweets of knowledge are unknown, and the terrors of ignorance hold their undisputed and remorseless reign. Sir, the laws recorded in the statute books of the free States, providing the means of education, and wooing the children to receive the blessedness of true knowledge, are worthy to be inscribed as emblems and hyeroglyphics upon the golden gates of Heaven; but those laws which deform the statute books of the slave States of this Union, making it a penal offence to educate human beings, and dooming immortal souls to perpetual ignorance, would make the most appropiate adornment wherewith to embellish with inscription and bas-relief the pillars of the council-hall of pandemonium.

Sir, if there is anything for which I would go back to childhood, and live this weary life over again, it is for the burning, exalting, transporting thrill and extacy with which the young faculties hold their earliest communion with knowledge. When the panting and thirsting soul first drinks the delicious waters of truth; when the moral and intellectual tastes and desires first seize the fragrant fruits that flourish in the garden of knowledge; then does the child catch a glimpse and foretaste of Heaven. He regales himself upon the nectar and ambrosia of the gods. Late in life, this zest is rarely if ever felt so keenly as at the beginning. Such ought not to be the fact; but our bodies are so systematically abused by transgressions of the laws of health and life, that the sympathizing soul loses the keenness of its early relish. Even then, however, age has its compensations. The old may experience the delights of learning, anew, in the reflex pleasure of seeing children learn. But these lofty and enduring satisfactions,—this pleasure, it is no extravagance to say, this bliss of knowledge, both for parent and child, is withheld, cruelly, remorselessly withheld from the slave. We know all this; we see its imbruting consequences; and we are compelled to see them, because the Government will uphold slavery here.

Such, sir, is the spectacle which is presented to all northern men, whenever for duty, for business, for pleasure, they visit this metropolis. Wherever we go, wherever we are, the odious, abhorred concomitants of this institution are forced upon our observation, and become a perpetual bitterness in the cup of life. The whole system, with all its adjuncts, is irreconcilably repugnant to our ideas of justice. We believe it to be a denial of the rights of man; we believe it to be contrary to the law of God. Whether these feelings wear away by the lapse of time, and the indurating power of custom, I know not; but, for one, I hope never to become hardened and callous to the sight; for it is a case where I could experience no mitigation of my pains, without a corresponding debasement of my nature.

THE WHOLE COUNTRY RESPONSIBLE.

Now, in all sincerity, and in all kindness, I ask our southern brethern, what there is to them so valuable and desirable in retaining slavery here, as to be a compensation for all the pain and evil which its existence inflicts upon the North? Surely its abandonment here would be a small thing to them, while its continuance is a great thing to us, because we are held responsible for it by the whole civilized world. This District is the common possession of the nation. Congress has power of exclusive legislation over it. Congress, therefore, is responsible for its institutions as a man is responsible for the condition of his house, and the custom of his family. The general government is not responsible for the local institutions of Massachusetts or of Mississippi. Each of them has supreme control over its own domestic concerns. They may honorably discharge their debts or repudiate them; they may build up institutions of charity, of learning, and of religion; or they may suffer inhumanity and violence, ignorance and paganism, to prevail; and we, here, cannot help it, and therefore are not responsible for it. But it is wholly otherwise with regard to the institutions that prevail in this District; their honor, or their infamy attaches to us. We are judged by them the world round. We of the northern States feel it at home; we are made to feel it still more deeply abroad. Throughout every nation in Europe, it is the common language and the common sentiment, that an institution which exists in one half of the States of this Union is in flagrant contrast and contradiction to the theory of our Government. When we are reminded of this,—whether in a kindly and expostulatory manner by our friends, or in an offensive and taunting one by our enemies, we of the North can say, at least, that we are not responsible for it. We can explain why we are no more amenable for the local laws of Arkansas or Missouri, than we are for the Catholic religion in Mexico, or for the revolutions in the South American republics. This is our answer. But they still retort upon us, and say, There is one spot for which you are responsible,—the District of Columbia. You could abolish slavery there if you would; you do not; and therefore the sin of its continuance is yours, as much so as if it existed in New York or Massachussetts. Now, I ask southern gentlemen how it is consistent with magnanimity and honor, with a fraternal feeling towards the North, for them to force the odium of this inconsistency upon us? Surely they gain no credit, no character by it; we lose both credit and character. The existence of slavery here is no benefit to them; it is of unspeakable injury to us. They would lose nothing by surrendering it, we suffer everything by its continuance.

A change would work them no injury ; it would be invaluable to us. I ask them on principles of common fairness and good neighborhood, that they should courteously and voluntarily yield us this point, which would allay so much bitterness and heart-burning at the North, and which, according to their view of the matter, would fill the South with the sweet savor of a generous deed.

I know, sir, that some southern gentlemen profess to see a principle in such a course that debars them from adopting it. They say that if slavery in this District should be surrendered, it would only be giving the adversary a vantage ground, on which he could plant himself to attack slavery in the State. I dissent from this view entirely. Has not the gentleman from Ohio, (Mr. Giddings,) who is supposed to represent the extreme anti-slavery views which exist in this House,—has he not declared here, a hundred times over, that he disclaims all right, that he renounces all legal authority and pretext, under the Constitution, to lay the hands of this Government, for the purpose of freeing him, on a single slave in the slave States? But clearly the principle is different in regard to slaves in this District, where we possess the power of " exclusive legislation." But if gentlemen at the South see a principle which debars them from surrendering slavery in this District, we at the North see a principle which prompts us and will prompt us, until the work is accomplished, to renewed exertions. On the same ground on which slavery in this District has been defended for the last fifty years, it can be defended for the next fifty, or the next five hundred years; it can be defended forever. This idea of perpetual slavery in the very household of a republic of freemen, is not to be tolerated, and cannot be tolerated. But I will not dwell on this topic further. I close this branch of my argument with a proposition which seems to me but fair and equitable. The South has held this metropolis as a slave capital for fifty years. Let it now be held as a free capital for fifty years; and if, at the end of this period, adequate reasons can be shown, before any nation, civilized or uncivilized, upon the face of the earth, for restoring it to slavery again, I for one, should have no fears of entering into an engagement upon such a condition, that it should again become " a land of Egypt and a house of bondage."

Notwithstanding I have dwelt so long upon the social and moral aspects of this subject, I am still tempted not to forego that which was my principal object in rising, namely, to submit an argument on the question of the legality or constitutionality of slavery in this District. I have bestowed much careful attention upon this subject, with the sincerest desire of arriving at true, legal, and constitutional results. I submit my views with deference, because I know they are in conflict with the views of others for whose knowledge and abilities I have the profoundest respect.

The legality of slavery in the District of Columbia has been assumed, and practically acquiesced in, for fifty years. Had the question of its validity been raised, and argued on the principles of the Constitution, immediately after the creation of the District, I believe this territory would have been declared free soil. In my conscientious opinion, slavery exists in this District only by original usurpation and subsequent acquiescence. If so, Congress cannot be too speedily invoked to abdicate the power it has usurped.

FIRST ARGUMENT AGAINST ITS LEGALITY.

The first position I take is this, THAT SLAVERY HAS NO LEGAL EXISTENCE, UNLESS BY FORCE OF POSITIVE LAW.

If any man claims authority over the body, mind and soul of one of his fellow-men, and claims this authority not only for the whole life of his victim, but a like authority over all his descendants, there is no part of the civilized world where he will not be required to show some positive law, authorizing the power and the bondage. If the claimant says, " I am stronger, or I am wiser than he ;" or " I have an Anglo-Saxon brain, while he has only an African brain ;" or " my skin is white and his skin is not white ;" or " I descended from Shem and he from Ham ; and, therefore he is my slave," —there is not a court in Christendom, which, though it may admit the fact, will ratify the inference. If the claimant affirms that it is *morally* right for him to seize his fellow-man and reduce him to slavery ; if he brings the Bible into court as his law-book, and cites Abraham and Isaac and Jacob and Paul, as his authorities ; still, I say, there is not a court in Christendom that will not deny the validity of the title, and rebuke the arrogance of the demand.* Positive law, then, is the only foundation of slavery. The authorities are numerous, if not numberless, to establish this position. I shall not incumber this argument by citing many of them. The few which I shall cite will contain a reference to the rest.

The grand reason against slavery given by Lord Mansfield, in Somersett's case, was, " that it is so intrinsically wrong that it is incapable of being introduced into any country, or any reasons moral or political, and can only stand on positive law." (20 State Trials, J.)

Chief Justice Marshall says, " that it [slavery] is contrary to the law of nature, will scarcely be denied. That every man has a natural right to the fruits of his own labor, is generally admitted ; and that no other person can rightfully deprive him of those fruits and appropriate them against his will, seems to be the necessary result of this admission." (Antelope, 10 Wheat., 120.)

" The first objection," says Mr. Justice Best, in the case of

that it does not appear, in the special case, that the right to slaves exists in East Florida. *That right is not a general but a local right ;* it ought, therefore, to have been shown that it existed in Florida, and that the defendants knew of its existence. Assuming, however, that those facts did appear, still, under the circumstances of this case, this action could not be maintained.

" The question is, were these persons slaves at the time when Sir G. Cockburn refused to do the act which he was desired to do ? I am decidedly of opinion that they were no

* An anecdote, which I have on the best authority, is not inappropriate. A few years ago, a citizen of the State of Connecticut absconded, leaving a wife behind him. He went to the State of Mississippi, where he took a coloured woman as his concubine, had children by her, acquired property, and died. The wife and heirs in Connecticut claimed the property acquired in Mississippi. The claim was contested. The honorable. Henry S. Foote, now a Senator from that State, conducted the defence. He denied the title of the wife in Connecticut, affirmed that of the concubine and her children in Mississippi, and cited the case of Abraham and Sarah and Hagar, to prove the legality and the propriety of the concubinage, and the Divine authority for it. And surely, if the Bible argument in favor of slavery is sound, Mr. Foote's argument in favor of concubinage is equally so.

longer slaves. The moment they put their feet on board a *British* man-of-war, not lying within the waters of East Florida, (where undoubtedly the laws of that country would prevail,) those persons who had before been slaves were free. * * * Slavery is a local law, and therefore, if a man wishes to preserve his slaves, let him attach them to him by affection, or make fast the bars of their prison, or rivet well their chains; *for the instant they get beyond the limits where slavery is recognized by the local law, they have broken their chains, they have escaped 'from their prison, and are free."* (2 Barn. & Cres., 466–7, Forbes *vs.* Cochrane, S. C., 3 Dowl. and Ryland, 679.)

"I am of opinion," says Holroyd, J., in the same case, " that according to the principles of the English law, the right to slaves, even in a country where such rights are recognized by law, must be considered as founded, not upon the law of nature, but upon the particular law of that country."

" The law of slavery is a law *in invitum ; and when a party gets out of the territory where it prevails,* and of the power of his master, and gets under the protection of another power, without any wrongful act done by the party giving that protection, the right of the master, *which is founded on the municipal law of the particular place only,* does not continue, and there is no right of action against a party who merely receives the slave in that country, without doing any wrongful act.".

The definition of slavery given by the Roman law implies that it is local : *Servitus est constitutio juris gentium qua quis dominio alienio,* CONTRA NATURAM, *subjicitur.* 18 Pick. Rep., 193, Commenwealth *vs.* Aves. Lunsford *vs.* Coquillon, 14 Martin's Rep. 402. "The relation of owner and slave is a creation of the municipal law." 3 Marshall, 470, Ky., Ran-. Hopper.

4 Wash. C. C.   immons. 9 Curry's Louisiana

This point may be presented in another light. By the law of nature all men are free. But in some Governments the law of the State, upheld by the power of the State, overrides the law of nature, and enslaves a portion of the people. The law of nature recedes before this legalized violence; but it recedes no further than the legalized violence drives it back. Within the jurisdictional limits of such States, then, slavery is made *legal*, though it is not made *right*. But if a slave passes out of the jurisdiction where violence overpowers right, into a jurisdiction where right is superior to violence, he is then free; not because there is any change in the man, but because there is a change in the laws to which the man is subject.

There may, however, be some further positive law which, though it does not authorize the buying or selling of a slave, still does provide that an escaped or escaping slave may be recaptured and redelivered into bondage. Such is the third paragraph of the second section of the fourth article of the Constitution of the United States. Such, too, is the act of Congress of February 12, 1793, providing for the recapture of fugitive slaves. This, however, would not be without positive law.

The debates in all the conventions for adopting the Constitution of the United States, proceed upon the ground that slavery depends upon positive law for its existence. If it did not,—if a man who has a legal right to a slave in Virginia, has a legal right to him anywhere, then the provision in the Constitution, and the act of 1793, for recapturing fugitive slaves, would have been unnecessary.

On the south side of a boundary line, then, slavery may exist by force of positive law; while, on the north side, in the absence of any such law, slavery is unlawful. A slave passing out of a jurisdiction where slavery is legalized, into a jurisdiction where it is not, becomes free. It is as though a man should migrate from one of those South Sea islands, where cannibalism is legalized, and where the public authorities, according to the reports of travellers, not only condemn and execute a criminal, *but dine on him, after he is executed,* —it is I say as though the subject of such a government, should migrate into one where cannibalism is not lawful, and where therefore, though he should be condemned and executed for crime, it would be no part of the sentence or the ceremony that he should be eaten. He is out of cannibal jurisdiction.

The right of freedom is a natural right. It is a positive existence. It is a moral entity. Like the right to life, it pertains, by the law of nature and of God, to every human being. This moral right continues to exist until it is abolished. Some act abolishing this freedom, then, must be proved;

it must be proved affirmatively, cr else the fact of freedom remains. This is the solid and indestructible ground of the maxim, that slavery can exist only by positive law; that it is a *local* institution; that the right of freedom must first be abolished before slavery can exist.

SECOND ARGUMENT.

My second position is this: *That a man's legal condition may be changed by a change in the Government over him, while he remains in the same place, just as effectually as it can be changed by his removal to another place, and putting himself under another government.* The inhabitants of the North American colonies did not change their place of residence when they passed from under the government of Great Britain, and came under the Government of the Confederation. The Mexicans, inhabiting the then States of California and New Mexico, did not change their place of residence, when, on the thirtieth day of May last, they ceased to be citizens of the Mexican Republic, and became citizens, or *quasi* citizens of the United States. Their political relations were changed, not by their removal from under the canopy of one government and placing themselves under the canopy of another government, but by the withdrawal of one government from over them, and by the extension to them of certain *political* rights and capacities under another government. Before this thirtieth day of May, they could have committed treason against Mexico, but not after it. Before it they could not commit treason against the United States; but when they shall be citizens of the Union, they can. These vital changes in their relations are without any change in their residence. Within my recollection, an old gentleman died in Massachusetts, who had lived in five different towns, but still remained where he was born, like one of the old oak trees, on the old homestead. The part of the original town where he was born had been set off and incorporated into a new town; and that part of the second town where he lived, into a third; and so on, until he died in the fifth town, without any change of domicil. Now, this man lived under the jurisdiction and by-laws of five towns, as they were successively incorporated over him, just as much as though he had struck his tent five times, and placed himself, by successive migrations, under five different municipal jurisdictions.

A similar thing must have happened to thousands of our
fellow-citizens of the Union : some of them at first lived under a foreign government ; then under one territorial government ; then under another ; and at last have become citizens
of a State, without any change of domicil.   Indeed, it would
seem that nothing can be clearer than the proposition, whether
regarded as a legal or a political one, than that the laws and
the jurisdiction may be changed over a man who continues
to reside in the same place, just as effectually and as com-
pletely as a man may change the laws and jurisdiction over
himself by removing to a different place.   In many cases, the
former works a more thorough change than the latter.   The
laws of great Britain do not acknowledge the right of self-ex-
patriation ; while, at the same time, it is held, that the inhabitants of a foreign province, incorporated into the king-
dom, change their allegiance without changing their residence.

THIRD ARGUMENT.

My third proposition is this : *That the jurisdiction under
which the inhabitants of what is now the District of Columbia
lived, prior to the cession of the District of Maryland to the
United States, was utterly and totally changed, at the moment
of the cession,—at the moment when, according to the provi-
sions of the Constitution, they ceased to be citizens of the
State of Maryland, and became citizens of the District of
Columbia.*

By the 17th paragraph (Hickey's Constitution) of the 8th
section of the 1st article, it is provided that Congress shall
have power to exercise exclusive legislation in all cases whatsoever over such District, (not exceeding ten miles square,)
as may, by cession of particular States, and the acceptance of
Congress, become the seat of the government of the United
States.

Congress, then, has the power of sole and exclusive legislation " in all cases whatsoever," in regard to the District of
Columbia.   What is the meaning of the word "exclusive"
in this connection ?   It cannot mean *absolute* and *uncontrolled ;*
for, if it did, it would make Congress as sovereign as the
Russian autocrat.   It means that no other government, no
other body of men whatever, shall have concurrent power of
legislation over the District ; nor, indeed, any subordinate

power, except what may be derived from Congress. Over every man who is a citizen of one of the United States, there are two jurisdictions,—the jurisdiction of the General Government, and the jurisdiction of the State Government. There are two governments that have the power to legislate for him; but there is only one power,—the Congress of the United States,—that can legislate for a citizen of the District of Columbia.

In Kendall *vs.* the United States, 12 Peters, 524, it is said: " There is in the District of Columbia no division of powers between the general and State governments. Congress has the entire control over the District, for every purpose of government."

So it has been held that a justice of the peace in the District of Columbia is an officer of the government of the United States, and is therefore exempt from militia duty. Wise *vs.* Withers, 3 Crash, 331 ; 1 Cond. Rep. 552.

A citizen of the District of Columbia is not a citizen of any one of the United States. Hepburn *et. al. vs.* Ellery, 2 Cranch 445; Westcott's Lessee *vs.* Inhabitants ————, Peters' C. C. R., 45.

Up to the time of the cession, the inhabitants of this District were under two jurisdictions—that of Maryland, and that of Congress; but after the cession, under that of Congress alone. Now, when the inhabitants of this District passed out of the jurisdiction of Maryland, and came under the exclusive jurisdiction of Congress, let us see what was the effect of such change of jurisdiction upon them.

In the act of Congress of 1790, chap. 28, sect. 1, which was an act for establishing the seat of government of the United States, there is the following clause: "*Provided, nevertheless*, That the operation of the laws of the State [of Maryland] within such District shall not be effected by this acceptance, *until the time fixed for the removal of the government thereto, and until Congress shall, otherwise by law provide.*"

Here, then, Congress *expressly* provided and contracted with the State of Maryland, that the laws of Maryland in this District should not be interfered with, until the removal of the seat of government to this place ; and Congress likewise *impliedly* provided and contracted, that when the seat of government should be removed to this place, it would discharge the duty imposed upon it by the Constitution of the United States, and would assume and exercise the "exclusive legislation" provided for in that instrument. This act of Congress was approved on the 16th of July, 1790.

By the Maryland laws of 1791, chap. 45, sec. 2, that State ceded to the United States that territory which now constitutes the District of Columbia, and the words of the cession are these: "in full and absolute right, as well of soil as of person, residing or to reside therein," &c. * * * provided that the jurisdiction of the laws of Maryland "shall not cease or determine *until Congress shall by law provide for the government thereof*."

The state of the case, then, was simply this: 1. The Constitution gave Congress power of "exclusive legislation" over such district as might be ceded for the seat of government. 2. Congress, by the act of 1790, above referred to, proposed to the State of Maryland to accept a portion of her territory for this purpose, but engaged not to interfere with her laws until after it had taken actual possession of the ceded territory. 3. Maryland accepted the proposition, rehearsing the condition in these words, namely, that "the laws of Maryland shall not cease or determine until Congress shall by law provide for the government thereof."

By the 6th section of the act of 1790, chap. 28, Congress provided that it would remove to this District, and make this the seat of government, on the first Monday of December, 1800. It did so; and both its express duty under the constitution, and its implied promise to the State of Maryland, were to be fulfilled, by exercising "exclusive legislation over this district."

In fulfilment of this duty and promise, Congress, on the 27th of February, 1801, by the act of 1801, ch. 15, proceeded to legislate for the District of Columbia; and in the first section of that act, it provided as follows:

"*Be it enacted*, &c., That the laws of the State of Virginia, as they now exist, shall be and continue in force in that part of the District of Columbia, which was ceded by the said State to the United States, and by them accepted for the permanent seat of Government; and that the laws of the State of

State to the United States, and by them accepted, as afore-
said."
* By this act, then, Congress assumed to exercise, and did
exercise, that exclusive legislation over the District of Columbia, which had been provided for by the Constitution.

That portion of the District which was ceded to Congress
by Virginia, having been receded to that State by the act of
Congress of July 9, 1846, (st. 1846, chap. 35,) all that relates
to it may, for the purposes of this argument, be laid out of the
question.

On the 27th day of February, 1801, then, the laws of
Maryland, *as such*, were abrogated in this district. The
legislative power of Congress became exclusive. All legislative power previously possessed by Maryland over it then
ceased. The connection of Maryland with this District, as
a part of its lormer territory, and occupied by its former citizens, was dissolved. It had no longer any more legislative
power over the District than Maine or Georgia had. Histo-
rically, we may talk about the laws of Maryland, as they
once existed here ; but practically, and as a matter of strict
law and fact, her laws were no longer known within the
District. The laws which governed the people of this Dis-
after the 27th day of February, 1801, were the laws of Congress, and not the laws of Maryland.

To show that this part of the District passed out from
under the government of Maryland, and came under the government of the United States, I refer to Reilly, appellant,
vs. Lamar, *et. al.*, 2d Cranch 344, 1 Cond. Rep. 322, where
it is said, "By the separation of the District of Columbia
from the State of Maryland, the residents in that part of Maryland which became a part of the District, ceased to be citizens
of the State. It was held, in that case, that a citizen of the
District of Columbia could not be discharged by the insolvent
law of Maryland.

A citizen of the District of Columbia cannot maintain an
action in the circuit court of the United States out of the
District, he not being a citizen of the State within the meaning of the provision of the law of the United States regulating
the jurisdiction of the courts of the United States. Hepburn
et. al. vs. Ellzey, 2 Cranch, 445, 1st Cond. Rep., 444. See
also Loughborough *vs.* Blake, 5 Wheat., 317, and Levy Court
of Washington *vs.* Ringgold, 5 Peters, 451.

FOURTH ARGUMENT.

The next point of inquiry is, *what is the legal 'force and effect upon the subject of slavery, of the act of Congaess of 1801, before cited:* "That the laws of the State of Maryland, as they now exist, shall be continued in force in that part of said District which was ceded by that State to the United States," &c. And here I acknowledge that the operation of this clause is precisely the same as though Congress had transcribed all the Maryland laws, word for word, and letter for letter, into its own statute book, with the clause prefixed, "Be it enacted by the Senate and House of Representatives of the United States of America in Congress assembled," and the President of the United States had affixed his signature thereto. I acknowledge further, that the laws of Maryland had legalized slavery within the State of Maryland, and had defined what classes of persons might be held as slaves therein.

But it by no means follows, because Congress proposed to re-enact, in terms, for this District, all the laws of Maryland, that, therefore, it did re-enact them. It does not follow, that because two Legislatures use the same words they must necessarily have the same effect. It makes all the difference in the world, whether words are used by one possessed of power, or by one devoid of power. Congress might pass a law in precisely the same words used by the Parliament of Great Britain, and yet the law of Congress be invalid and inoperative, while

a written constitution; Great Britain has no written constitution. The British Parliament, on many subjects, has an ampler jurisdiction than the American Congress. The law of Congress might be unconstitutional and void, while that of the British Parliament, framed in precisely the same language, might be constitutional and binding.

So the law of.Maryland might be valid under the constitution of Maryland, and therefore binding upon the citizens of Maryland; while the law of Congress, though framed in precisely the same words, would be repugnant to the Constitution of the United States, and therefore have no validity.

Now, this is precisely the case here. Congress, in attempting to re-enact the Maryland laws, to uphold slavery in this District, transcended the limits of its constitutional power. It acted unconstitutionally. It acted in plain contravention of some of the plainest and most obvious principles consecrated by the constitution. If so, no one will dispute that its act is void. I do not deny then, that Congress used words of sufficient amplitude to cover slavery ; but what I deny is, that it had any power to give legal force to those words.

FIFTH ARGUMENT.

My next proposition, therefore, is this : that *as Congress can do nothing excepting what it is empowered to do by the Constitution, and as the Constitution does not empower it to establish slavery here, it cannot establish slavery here, nor continue it.*

Where is there any *express* power given to Congress by the Constitution to establish slavery ? Where is the article, section, or clause? I demand to have the title shown. Thousans of human beings are not to be robbed of all their dearest rights ; and they and their children, forever, by strained constructions, or apocryphal authority, doomed to bondage. Will those who say that Congress cannot establish a banking institution by construction, nor aid internal improvements, nor enact a tariff—will they say that can make a man a slave, and all his posterity slaves, by construction ?

Nor can any power to establish slavery be deduced from the 18th clause of the 8th section of the 1st article of the Constitution, which gives Congress power "to which shall be necessary and proper for carrying into execution" the powers that are granted.

What power is granted to Congress, for the exercise of which, the establishment of slavery in this District is a necessary means or preliminary ? Congress has power to lay and collect taxes; to borrow money ; to regulate commerce; to establish uniform rules of naturalization ; to coin money ; to punish counterfeiters ; to establish post offices and post roads ; to promote the progress of science and the arts ; to establish courts; to define and punish piracies on the high seas ; to declare war, to raise and support armies ; to provide and maintain a navy; to organize and maintain a militia ; and so forth, and so forth. But to what one of all these powers, is the power to establish slavery in the District of Columbia a necessary incident ? If slavery in the District of Columbia were to cease to-day, could not the government continue to exercise every function which it has heretofore exercised? If so, then the existence of slavery in this District is not "necessary" to the exercise of any of the power expressly granted. I call upon any gentleman to name any one power of this government which cannot be exercised, which must necessarily cease, if slavery should cease to be, in this District of Columbia? I must pause for a reply.

Well, then, if a power to establish slavery in this District is not among the granted powers, and if it is not necessary for the exercise of any of the granted powers, then it is nowhere,—it does not exist at all. No power of Congress, then, exists, either for the creation or for the continuance of slavery in this District: and all the legislation of Congress upon this subject is beyond or against the Constitution.

FURTHER ILLUSTRATION.

Let me illustrate this in another way. Suppose there had been a religious establishment in Maryland at the time of the cession; suppose, under the auspices of Lord Baltimore, the Catholic religion had been established as the religion of the State ; and that, in order to punish heresy and secure conformity to the religion of the State, an inquisition had been founded, and that the seat of that inquisition had been within the limits of the District of Columbia, at the time of the cession ; could Congress, in the absence of all express or implied authority on the subject of establishing a State religion, have upheld the Catholic religion here, and appointed the officers of the inquisition to administer it? The idea is abhorent to the whole spirit of the Constitution. But Congress had as much power to establish a national religion here, in the absence of all express or implied authority to do so, as to establish slavery here.

Congress, then, does not and cannot legalize slavery in this District. It found slavery in existence in the States; and it does not abolish it, or interfere with it, because it has no power of "exclusive legislation" in them. But Congress has as much right to go into any State and abolish slavery there, as any State, even Virginia or Maryland, has to come into this District with its laws and establish slavery here. I suppose that no jurist will contend that Congress could have passed the act of 1793, for the recapture of fugitive slaves, had it not been for the third clause in the second section of

the fourth article of the Constitution, which provides for the
re-delivery of a fugitive slave, on the claim of his master.
By this article in the Constitution, the case of *fugitive* slaves
only is provided for. If a master voluntarily carries his slave
into a free State, and the slave departs from his possession, he
cannot reclaim him. Why not? Why cannot Congress pass
a law, that if a man takes a dozen slaves to Boston, and they
there see fit to strike for wages, and to leave his possession
because their terms are not complied with,—why is it, I ask,
that Congress cannot pass a law authorizing their seizure and
delivery into the master's hands? The reason is, that the
Constitution has conferred upon Congress no such express
power, nor is any such power implied as being necessary to
the exercise of any power that is expressed. And if Congress
cannot so much as restore a slave to a master, who has voluntarily carried him into a free State, how can it continue
slavery in this District, after Maryland has ceded it to this
Government, whose fundamental, organic law gives it no
power to create or continue slavery here?

Suppose Maryland had ceded her share of the District to
Massachusetts, would not every slave in it have been instan-
taneously free by the Constitution of Massachusetts? They
would have been transferred to a free jurisdiction,—just as
much as an individual owner of a slave passes under a free
jurisdiction, when he voluntarily takes his slave to the North.
The legal existence of slavery was annulled in this District,
when Congress exercised its " exclusive " power over it, just
as much as the debtor's right to be discharged under the Maryland bankrupt law was annulled.

But I go further than this; and I say that the Constitution
not only does not empower Congress to establish or continue
slavery in this District, but again and again, by the strongest
implications possible, it prohibits the exercise of such a power.

In regard to this whole matter of slavery, the Constitution
touches the subject with an averted face. The abhorred word
"slave" is nowhere mentioned in it. The Constitution is asham-
ed to utter such a name. The country, coming fresh from that
baptism of fire—the American Revolution,—would not profane its lips with this unhallowed word. Hence, circumlo-
cution is resorted to. It seeks to escape a guilty confession.
Like a culprit, in whom some love of character still survives,
it speaks of its offence without calling it by name. It uses the

reputable and honorable word "persons," instead of the accursed word "slaves." As the Tyrian Queen, about to perpetrate a deed which would consign her character to infamy, called it by the sacred name of "marriage," and committed it,—

" Hoc prætexit nomine culpam ;"

so the Constitution about to recognize the most guilty and cruel of all relations between man and man, sought to avert its eyes from the act, and to pacify the remonstrances of conscience against every participation in the crime, by hiding the deed under a reputable word.

CONSTITUTIONAL PROHIBITION.

But let us look at the prohibitions of the Constitution; for I maintain that there is not only no power, express or implied, in the Constitution authorizing Congress to create or continue slavery in this District, but that it is debarred and prohibited from doing so, again and again.

I suppose no one will deny that the positive prohibitions, against the exercise of certain enumerated powers, apply to Congress, when legislating for this District, just as much as when legislating for the Union at large. This doctrine has recently been strongly asserted by Mr. Calhoun in the Senate of the United States; and, as I would gladly produce conviction in southern minds, I make use of this southern authority. He affirms that Congress, in legislating for the Territories, " is subject to many and important restrictions and conditions, of which some are expressed and others implied. Among the former may be classed all the general and absolute prohibitions of the Constitution ; that is, all those which prohibit the exercise of certain powers under any circumstances. In this class is included the prohibition of granting titles of nobility; passing *ex post facto* laws and bills of attainder ; the suspension of the writ of *habeas corpus*, except in certain cases ; making laws respecting the establishment of religion, or its free exercise, and every other of like description."

Will any man say that Congress can pass an *ex post facto* law for this District, and defend itself by referring to its power of exclusive legislation over it ? Can Congress pass a bill of attainder corrupting the blood of an inhabitant of this District, or repeal or suspend at any time, his right to a writ of *habeas corpus*, or establish a religion here, or interdict the free exercise thereof? No jurist, no statesman will pretend it.

But there is another prohibition in the Constitution every whit as full and explicit as any of these. The fifth article of amendment declares that "no person shall be deprived of life, liberty or property, without due process of law."

Here the Constitution uses the word "person," the most comprehensive word it could find. "No PERSON shall be deprived of life, liberty or property, without due process of law." Now, what does this word "person" mean? Or who, under the Constitution, is such a "person" as cannot be deprived of life, liberty, or property, by virtue of an act of Congress, *without due process of law?* Let us take our definition of the word "*person*" from the Constitution itself: "No *person* shall be a Representative, who shall not have attained the age of twenty-five years," &c., (see 2d clause of the 2d section of the 1st article.) "Representatives and direct taxes shall be apportioned among the several states which may be included within the Union, according to their respective numbers, which shall be determined by adding to the whole number of free *persons*, including those bound to service for a term of years, and excluding Indians not taxed, three-fifths of all other *persons*." (3d clause of the same section.) "No *person* shall be a Senator who shall not have attained the age of thirty years," &c., (1st art. 3d section, 3d clause.) "No *person* shall be convicted (of an impeachable offence, by the Senate,) without the concurrence of two-thirds," (1st article, 3d section, 6th clause.) "No *person* holding any office under the United States, shall be a member of either House, during his continuance in office," (1st article, 6th section, 2d clause.) "The migration or importation of such *persons* as any of the States now existing shall think proper to admit, shall not be prohibited"—"but a tax, or duty, may be imposed on such importation, not exceeding ten dollars for each *person*," &c., (1st article, 9th section, 1st clause.) "No *person* holding any office of profit or trust," "shall accept any present," &c., (1st article, 9th section, 8th clause.) "No *person* holding an office of trust or profit under the United States, shall be appointed an elector," (article 2, section 1, clause 2.) "The electors shall meet in their respective States, and vote by ballot for two *persons*," &c.

" The *person* having the greatest number of votes shall be the President, &c." " If no *person* have a majority," &c." " In every case, after the choice of the President, the *person* having the greatest number of votes of the electors, shall be Vice President," (article 2. section 1, clause 2.*) " No *person* except a natural born citizen," &c. " shall be eligible to the office of President: neither shall any *person* be eligible to that office, who has not attained the age of thirty-five years," &c. " No *person* shall be convicted of treason, unless on the testimony of two witnesses," &c., (article 3, section 3, clause 3.) A *person* charged in any State with treason," &c., (article 4, section 2, clause 2.) " No *person* held to service or labor," &c. (article 4, section 2, clause 3.)

Now, it will be seen from all this, that the word "*person*" is used in the Constitution in the most comprehensive sense. It embraces Indians, if taxed ; it embraces natives of Africa ; it embraces apprentices and slaves, or those held to service or labor ; and it embraces every citizen from the humblest to the highest, from the most true to the most treasonable. It embraces all, from the slave to the President of the United States.

And after having used the word to embrace all these classes and descriptions of men, it proceeds to say, in an amendment, that " *no* PERSON *shall be deprived of life, liberty or property, without due process of law.*" (Amendment, article 5.)

The law of Maryland ceded this District to Congress, " in full and absolute right, as well of soil as of *person*, residing or to reside therein."

Now Congress, in attempting to legalize slavery in the District of Columbia, has provided in terms, by its adoption of the Maryland laws, that one man may hold another man in bondage in this District, " WITHOUT DUE PROCESS OF LAW," and indeed without any process of law ; may hold him in bondage from his birth ; may beget him, and still hold him and his posterity in bondage. " Process of law" means legal proceedings. It is a phrase that does not pertain to the legislature, but to the courts. It means the institution of a suit in civil matters ; the finding of an indictment, or an information in criminal ones ; the issuing of subpœnas for witnesses, &c., in both. (See Art. 6 of Amendments to the Constitution.)

---

* This clause in the Constitution is annulled ; but for all purposes of determining the true interpretation of words, it is as good as ever.

Now, a slave is a *person* deprived of his liberty and property, without any process of law. There has been no " due" process of law to reduce him to this miserable condition ; there has been no process of law at all. A slave, therefore, in this District, is deprived of his liberty and property, in pursuance of the laws of Congress, without *any* legal process whatever, and therefore in flagrant contradiction of the fifth article of the Amendments to the Constitution of the United States. Hence, the act of congress, purporting to continue the Maryland laws respecting slavery in this District was, and is, and forever must be, until the Constitution is altered, null and void.

HISTORICAL FACT.

There is a striking historical fact in regard to the phraseology of this fifth article of amendment. Its substance was proposed by several States. Virginia proposed it in the following words : " No *freeman* ought to be taken, imprisoned, or dissiezed of his freehold liberties, privileges, or franchises, or outlawed or exiled, or in any manner destroyed or deprived of his life, liberty or property, but by the law of the land." (See 3 Elliott's debates, 593—Proceedings of June 27, 1788. Also, 4 Elliott's debates, 216, for the same amendment, as proposed by the State of New York.)

The Virginia amendment used the word " freeman." It proposed that no " freeman " should be deprived, &c. The New York amendment used the word " *person.*" And the amendment was adopted and ratified, almost in the words of the New York phraseology. The word *person* was chosen, and therefore Congress has no constitutional power to deprive of life, liberty, or property, *without due process of law,* any being embraced in the definition of that word. By its own selection of words, it is debarred not merely from depriving a " *freeman,*" but from depriving a " *person.*"

When Congress attempted to legalize and perpetuate slavery in this District, it violated the fourth article of the Amendments, which declares " the right of the people to be *secure* in their persons, houses, papers, and effects, against any unreasonable searches and seizures." If Congress cannot authorize domiciliary searches and seizures against a single individual, can it degrade a whole race of men to the condition of slaves, and then say that *because they are slaves,* they shall not be " secure ;" but shall be at the mercy of an alleged master, in regard to their persons—to be commanded or restrained, to be bought or sold? If Congress cannot authorize searches and seizures of houses, papers, and effects, can it get around the Constitution, by saying, we will create a class of persons who shall have no power of owning any houses, papers, or effects, to be searched or seized?

Again : Congress shall pass " no bill of attainder." What is a bill of attainder? It is a bill which works corruption of blood. It disfranchises its object. It takes away from him the common privileges of a citizen. It makes a man incapable of acquiring, inheriting, or transmitting property ; incapable of holding office, or acting as attorney for others ; and it shuts the door of the courts against him. These disabling couse-quences may descend to a man's children after him, though this is not necessary. Now, to pass such a bill, is a thing which Congress cannot do. But when Congress undertook to legalize slavery in this District, it undertook to do all this, and worse than all this. It attainted not individuals merely, but a whole race. A slave is an outlaw ; that is, he cannot make a contract; he cannot prosecute and defend in court; property cannot be acquired by him, or devised to him, or transmitted through him. A white man may give his testi-mony against him, but he cannot give his testimony against a white man. He is despoiled of his *liberam legem*—his birth-right. He cannot own the food or clothes he has earned. What is his, is his master's. And this corruption of blood, which the law of slavery works, does not stop with the first, nor with the second generation, nor with the tenth, nor the ten thousandth ; but by the theory of the law, goes on for ever. Bills of attainder, during the history of the worst pe-riods of the world, have applied to individuals only, or at most, to a family. But here, Congress, in defiance of the Con-stitution, has undertaken to establish a degraded caste in soci-ety, and to perpetuate it through all generations. Now, can any reasonable man for a moment suppose that the Constitu-tion meant to debar Congress from passing acts of attainder against individuals, but to permit it to pass wholesale, sweep-ing laws, working disfranchisements of an entire race, and en-tailing degradation for ever?

Let us look at another general prohibition of the Constitu-tion : " No title of nobility shall be granted by the United States, (art. 1, section 9, clause 8.) " The distinction of rank and honors," says Blackstone, "is necessary in every well-governed State, in order to reward such as are eminent for their services to the public." But the framers of the Constitution did not think so; the people of the United States did not think so; and therefore they incorporated a provision into their organic law, that "no title of nobility should be granted." But it matters not whether the favored individual is called "Marquis" or "Master." If he is invested by the Government with a monopoly of rights and privileges, in virtue of its title and its legal incidents, without any corresponding civil duties, he belongs to an order of nobility—he is a nobleman. Mr. McDuffie defends the institution of slavery, on the ground that it establishes the highest of all ranks and the broadest of all distinctions between men. He says no nation has yet existed which has not, in some form, created the distinction of classes, such as patrician and plebeian, or citizen and helot, or lord and commoner, and that the institution of slavery stands here instead of these orders, and supersedes them all. Now, is it not inconceivable that the Constitution should interdict the bestowment of special favors to distinguished individuals for meritorious services, and yet should authorize Congress to confer the highest of all earthly prerogatives—the prerogative over property, liberty, and volition itself, upon one class of men over another class of men? Yet, if Congress can create or legalize slavery, it can establish the worst order of nobility that ever existed. It can give to one class of men the power to own and to control, to punish and despoil another class; to sell father, mother, wife and children into bondage. To prohibit Congress from doing one of these things, and to permit it to do the other, is straining at a gnat while swallowing a camel—a whole caravan of camels.

But the same clause in the Constitution which gives Congress the power of exclusive legislation over this District, also empowers " to exercise like authority over all places purchased by the consent of the Legislature of the State, in which the same shall be, for the erection of forts, magazines, arsenals, dock yards, and other needful buildings." If, then, Congress has any constitutional power to legalize slavery in this District, it has the same power to legalize it (that is, to create it,) in all places in the State of Massachusetts, or New York, or any other, where it may have obtained territory from a State for a fort, magazine, arsenal, dock yard, or other needful building. Where it has obtained land in the middle of a city Philadelphia, New York, Boston, Chicago, for a custom house, it may create slavery there. The power to do this is conferred in precisely the same words as the power by which it has been held that slavery can be established in the District of Columbia.

And now I will occupy the few minutes that are left me in considering what seems to me the only plausible argument that can be urged in favor of the constitutionality of slavery in this District.

OBJECTION CONSIDERED.

It may be said, that when a Territory is obtained by one nation from another, whether by conquest or by treaty, the laws which governed the inhabitants at the time of the conquest or cession, remain in force until they are abrogated by the laws of the conquering or purchasing power. For this principle, the authority of Lord Mansfield, in the case of Campbell *vs.* Hall, 1 Cowper, 208, may be cited. The decision of our own courts are to the same effect. (See 2 Gallison's Reports, 561, United States, appt., *vs.* Juan Percheman ; 7 Peters, 51, Johnson *vs.* McIntosh ; 8 Wheat., 543.) I do not dispute the authority of this case. But it does not touch the question I am arguing ; or so far as it bears upon it at all, it confirms the views I would enforce. The principle is, that the existing laws remain in force *until* they are abrogated. I agree to this. But in the case of the District of Columbia, there was a special agreement between Maryland and the United States, that as soon as the United States should legislate for the District, the laws of Maryland, *as such*, should cease to be operative here. On the 27th day of February, 1801, therefore, all the rights which the citizens of this District possessed, they possessed under the law of Congress, and not under the law of Maryland. On the day preceding, a citizen could have voted for Governor or other State officers of Maryland ; on the day following, he could no longer vote for any such officer. On the day preceding, he could have voted for electors of President and Vice President of the United States ; on the day following, he was bereft of all such right of the elective franchise, and must accept such officers and legislators as the rest of the country might choose to elect for him. On the day preceding, he might, in the character of an insolvent debtor, have been discharged under the insolvent laws of Maryland; on the day following, he could no longer be so discharged. On the day preceding, he might have been required, through a justice of the peace of the State of Maryland, to perform militia duty ; but on the day following, if commissioned as a justice of the peace of the District of Columbia, he could not be compelled to perform militia duty, because he would, in such case, be an officer of the United States. On the day preceding, he might have sued in the circuit court of the United States, as being a citizen of Maryland ; but, on the day following, he could not so sue, because he had ceased to be a citizen of a State. Thus the change of jurisdiction over him deprived him of some privileges, and relieved him of some burdens. It deprived him of these privileges, and relieved him from these burdens, notwithstanding the act of Congress had said, in unambiguous words, " the laws of the State of Maryland, AS THEY NOW EXIST, *shall be and continue in'force* in that part of the said District which was ceded by that State to the United States." But the most momentous change which was wrought by the transfer of the citizen from the jurisdiction of Maryland to the jurisdiction of the United States, was that which made it impossible for him any longer to hold a slave. Under the laws of Maryland, he might have held his slave, for her statutes had legalized slavery ; but under the Constitution of the United States, he could not hold a slave ; for that constitution had given Congress no power to legalize slavery in this District, and had gone so far as to make prohibitions against it. His right to hold slaves then expired, or fell, like his right to vote for United States officers, or for State officers, or his right to be discharged under the Maryland insolvent law, or his right to sue in certain courts, &c., &c.

CONCLUSION.

One point more, sir, and I have done : Why, says my opponent, did not the right to hold slaves continue after the change of jurisdiction as well as the right to hold horses ? For the plainest of all reasons, I answer: for the reason that a horse is *property* by the universal consent of mankind, by the recognition of every civilized court in Christendom, without any positive law declaring it to be the subject of ownership ; but a *man* is not property, without positive law ; without a law declaring him to be the subject of ownership. There was such a positive law in Maryland; but Congress, for want of constitutional authority, could not enact, revive, or continue it. And such I verily believe would have been the decision of the Supreme Court of the United States, had the question been carried before them immediately subsequent to the act of 1801. But now, as slavery has existed practically in this District for half a century, it is proper to pass a law abolishing it.   It is better, under the present circumstances, that slavery should be abolished here by a law of Congress, than by the decision of a court ; because Congress can provide an indemnity for the owners, and let the slaves go free.   But should it be abolished by a legal adjudication, every slave would be hurried away to the South, and sold, he and his descendants, into perpetual bondage.

SPEECH

OF

HON. HORACE MANN,

OF MASSACHUSETTS,

ON

SLAVERY AND THE SLAVE-TRADE

IN THE

DISTRICT OF COLUMBIA,

DELIVERED IN THE HOUSE OF REPRESENTATIVES OF THE
UNITED STATES, FEBRUARY 23, 1849.

PHILADELPHIA:

MERRIHEW AND THOMPSON, PRINTERS,

No. 7 Carter's Alley.